WAS POCAHONTAS REAL?

BIOGRAPHY BOOKS FOR KIDS 9-12
CHILDREN'S BIOGRAPHY BOOKS

owner Holly C

BABY PROFESSOR
EDUCATION KIDS

Speedy Publishing LLC

40 E. Main St. #1156

Newark, DE 19711

www.speedypublishing.com

Copyright 2017

In this book, we're going to talk about the life of Pocahontas. So, let's get right to it!

WHO WAS POCAHONTAS?

There have been many books and films about the legend of Pocahontas. Some of the details in these stories are true and based on historical fact. However, as with all legends, some of the details of her life aren't known, so storytellers sometimes add fictional details.

CAPTAIN JOHN SMITH

Pocahontas was a real person. She was a Native American woman of the Powhatan tribe who became known for saving an Englishman by the name of John Smith. She also helped the English settlers who had populated the town of Jamestown in Virginia as they learned to live in the New World.

HER EARLY LIFE

Pocahontas was born in the land that is now eastern Virginia around 1595 AD. She was the daughter of a very important Native American chief, who was called Chief Powhatan after the name of their tribe. Her father was the chief not only of a tribe, but also of a large federation of tribes. They were living in the lands of Tidewater Virginia, which was called Tsenacommacah by the tribes. The tribes in this area spoke Algonquian.

COLONIAL NATIONAL HISTORICAL PARK,
JAMESTOWN, VIRGINIA

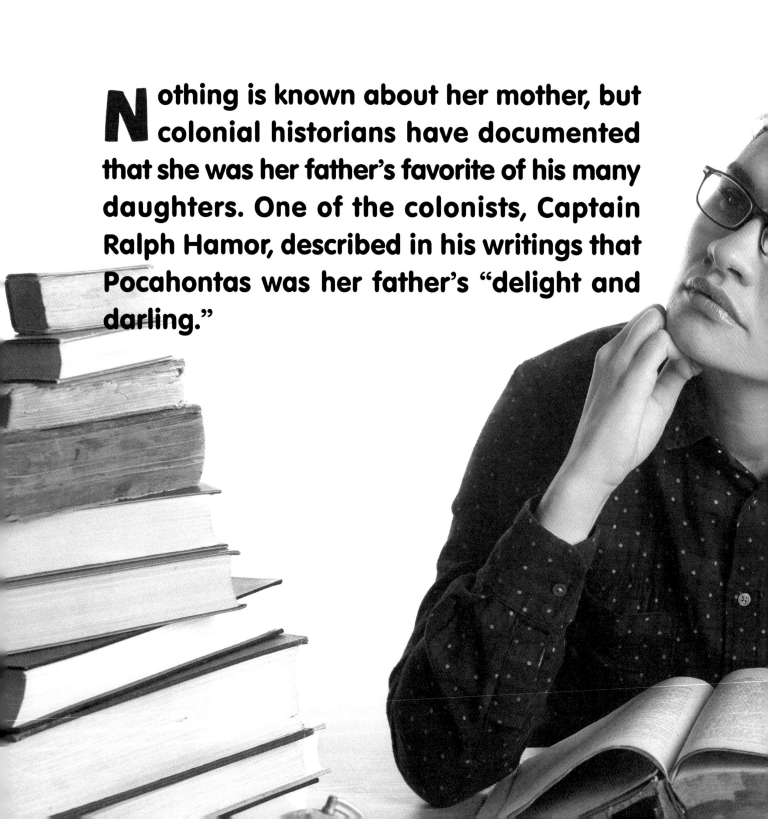

Nothing is known about her mother, but colonial historians have documented that she was her father's favorite of his many daughters. One of the colonists, Captain Ralph Hamor, described in his writings that Pocahontas was her father's "delight and darling."

Today we would say that she was the "apple of his eye" or his "little princess." However, as far as historians know, she wasn't officially a princess in the sense that she didn't have a regal or politically important position.

During her youth, she learned to hunt for food and collect firewood. More than likely she also learned some basic farming techniques and would have participated in building the tribe's thatched dwellings. She would have also been involved in preparing food and decorations for the tribal feasts.

THATCHED HUT

It was common for native people who spoke Algonquian to have numerous names that were used in different contexts. At one time in her youth she was called Matoaka. Later on, she was called Amonute. Her family probably called her by the name Pocahontas, which was a casual or endearing name. The name translates to "the spoiled child" or "the naughty one."

THE ARRIVAL OF THE ENGLISH SETTLERS

In 1607, Captain John Smith arrived on the shoreline of Virginia with a group of about one hundred other travelers. They started their settlement at Jamestown, an island that was very close to the Powhatan's lands. The colonists encountered the Tsenacommacah Indians on numerous occasions.

KNIGHT IN METAL ARMOR

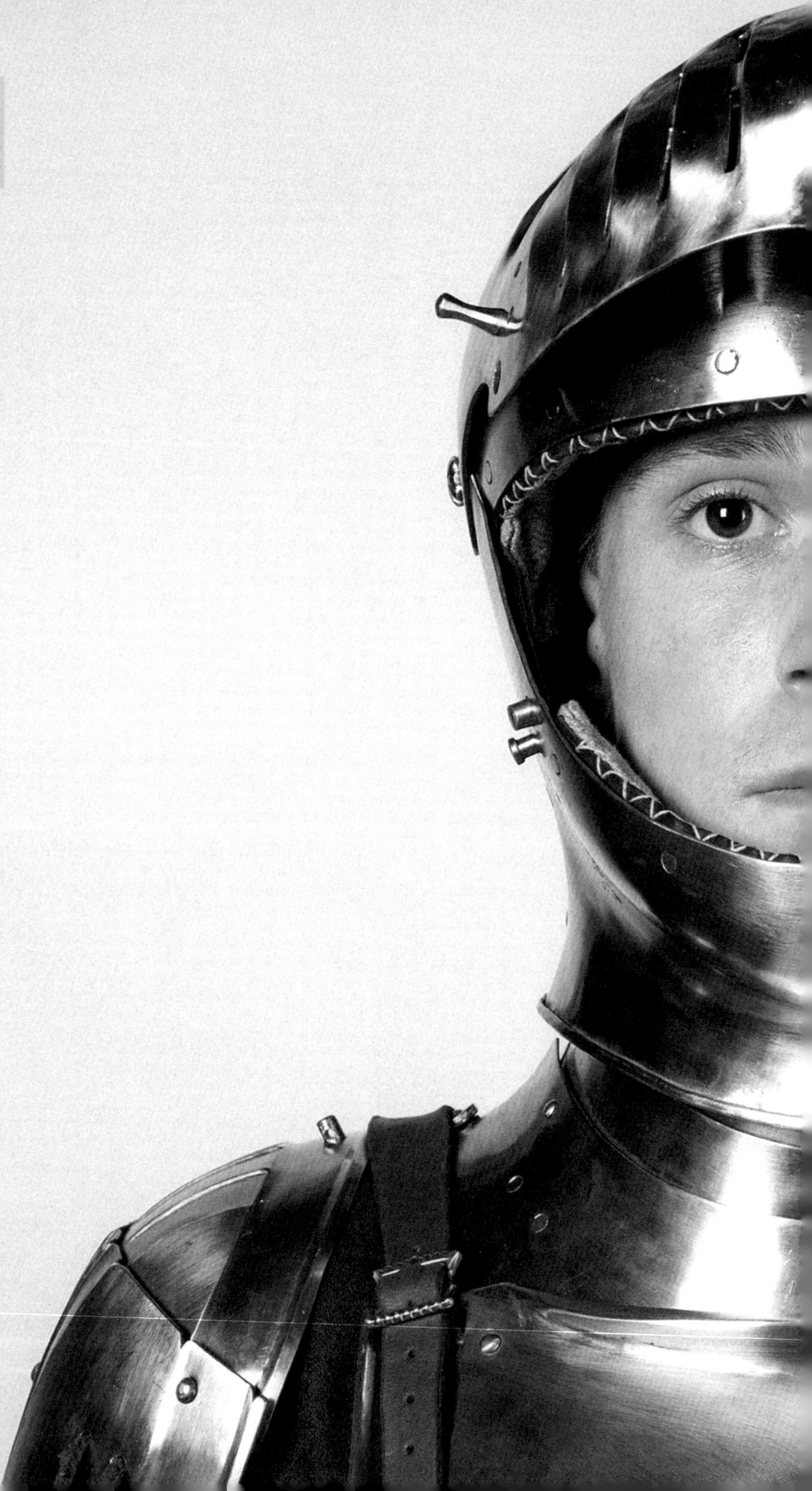

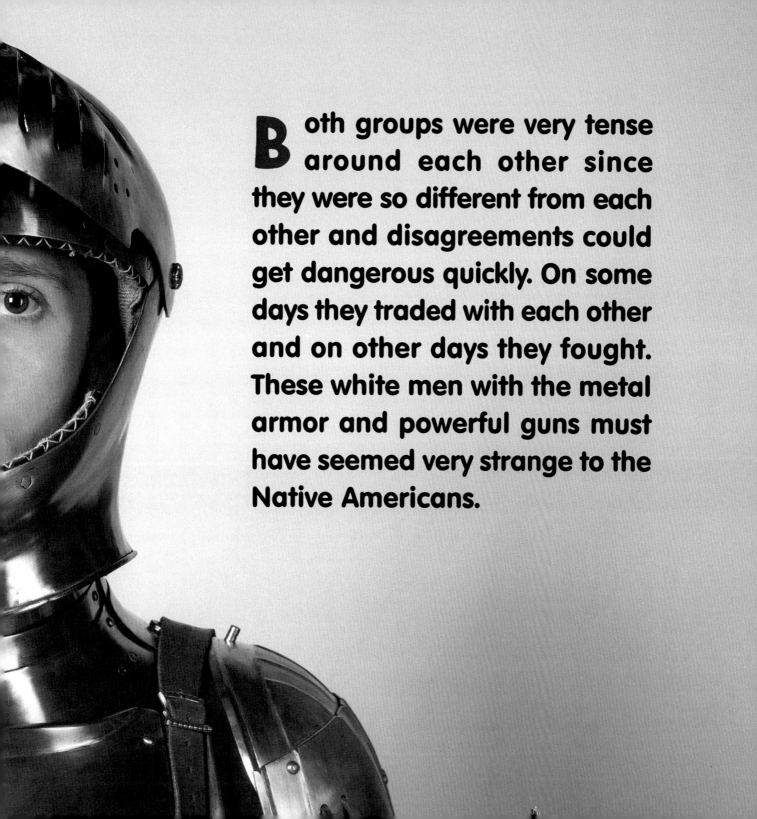

Both groups were very tense around each other since they were so different from each other and disagreements could get dangerous quickly. On some days they traded with each other and on other days they fought. These white men with the metal armor and powerful guns must have seemed very strange to the Native Americans.

In December of 1607, Captain John Smith was exploring the Chickahominy River when he was captured by some of the warriors led by Chief Powhatan. They brought John Smith to the chief's home. What happened next isn't exactly clear because John Smith wrote two different accounts of the history. In his first account, written in 1608, he said that he attended a large feast and spoke directly with the chief.

CHICKAHOMINY RIVER

QUEEN ANNE OF ENGLAND

In this first account of the history, Smith says he didn't meet Pocahontas until some months afterwards. However, later, in 1616, Captain Smith was asked to provide the history to Queen Anne of England. At that time, Queen Anne was waiting to meet Pocahontas and her husband.

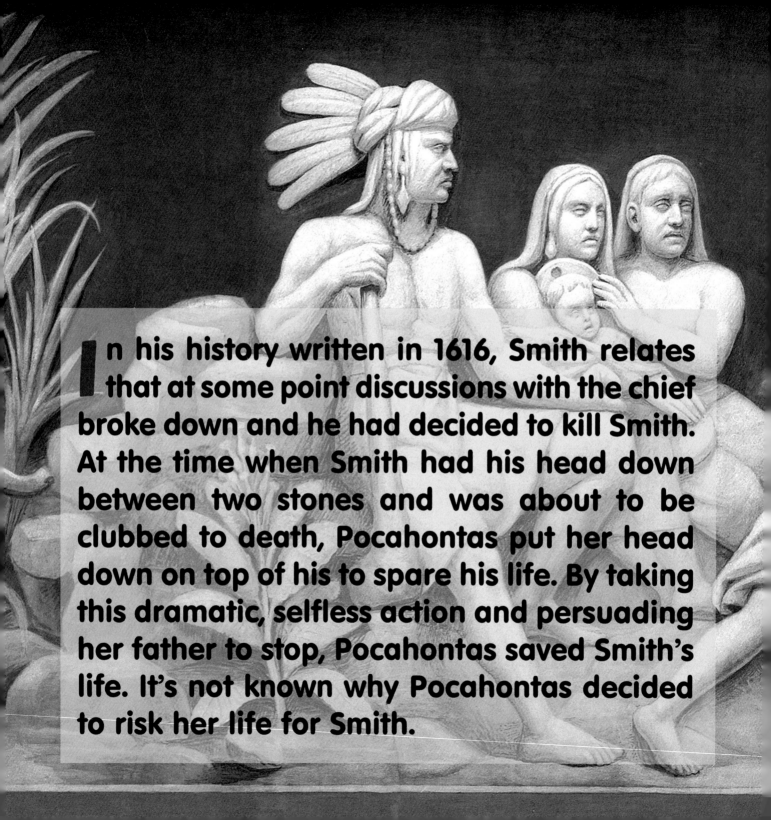

In his history written in 1616, Smith relates that at some point discussions with the chief broke down and he had decided to kill Smith. At the time when Smith had his head down between two stones and was about to be clubbed to death, Pocahontas put her head down on top of his to spare his life. By taking this dramatic, selfless action and persuading her father to stop, Pocahontas saved Smith's life. It's not known why Pocahontas decided to risk her life for Smith.

POCAHONTAS AT A YOUNG AGE

Later fiction stories tell of a romance between them, but there are no historical, factual details to prove that was true. Pocahontas was still a child of the age of twelve when this occurred.

Historians have debated for centuries as to whether this event actually happened or not. Some believe that John Smith thought he was to be killed when instead the chief and his warriors were going through a ritual to bring Smith in as an adopted member of their tribe. There's also a theory that Smith made up the story to ensure that Pocahontas was treated with respect within his group.

No matter what actually happened that fateful day, there are histories that establish that Smith and Pocahontas became friends and that she visited Jamestown quite frequently. When the colonists were on the brink of starvation, she brought them food and supplies.

FOOD SUPPLIES

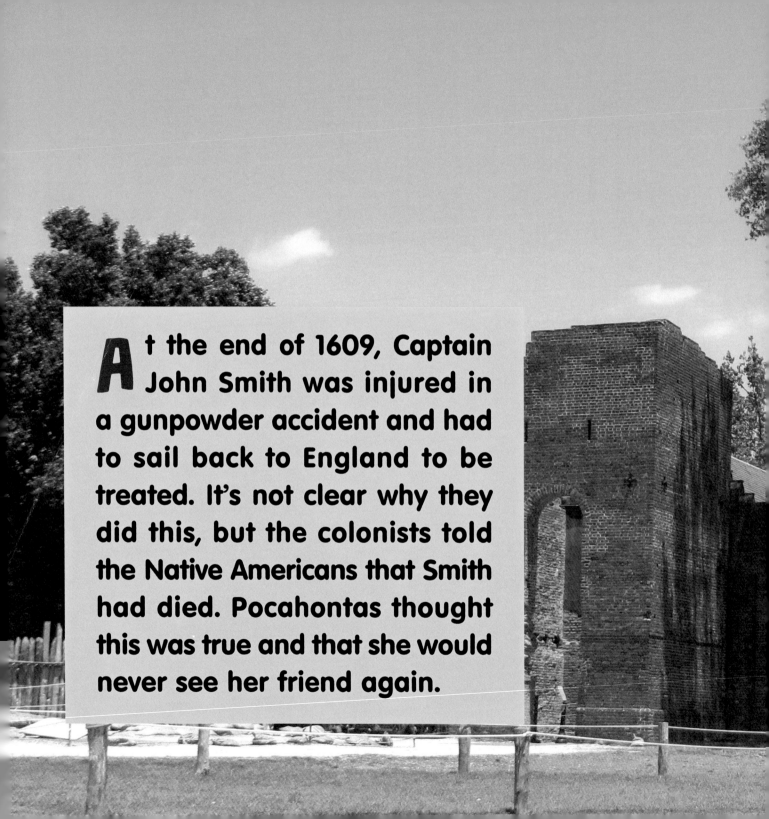

At the end of 1609, Captain John Smith was injured in a gunpowder accident and had to sail back to England to be treated. It's not clear why they did this, but the colonists told the Native Americans that Smith had died. Pocahontas thought this was true and that she would never see her friend again.

CAPTAIN
JOHN SMITH
GOVERNOR OF
VIRGINIA
1608

STATUE OF CAPTAIN JOHN SMITH

NATIVE AMERICAN WARRIOR

Around 1612, Pocahontas married a Native American warrior by the name of Kocoum. However, Pocahontas was not with him for long, because within a year she was captured.

POCAHONTAS IS CAPTURED

In 1613, a war broke out between the English settlers and the Powhatan tribe. The captain of Jamestown was Samuel Argall and he had formed an alliance with a group of Native Americans called the Patawomencks, who weren't loyal to the Powhatans.

CapitArgal

SAMUEL ARGALL WITH THE PATAWOMENCKS TRIBE

Argall and his followers thought they could use Pocahontas to negotiate with her father. They captured her and demanded a ransom from him. They wanted some of the English prisoners that Chief Powhatan was holding captive in exchange for her. It's not clear why this happened, but her father didn't give in to their demands.

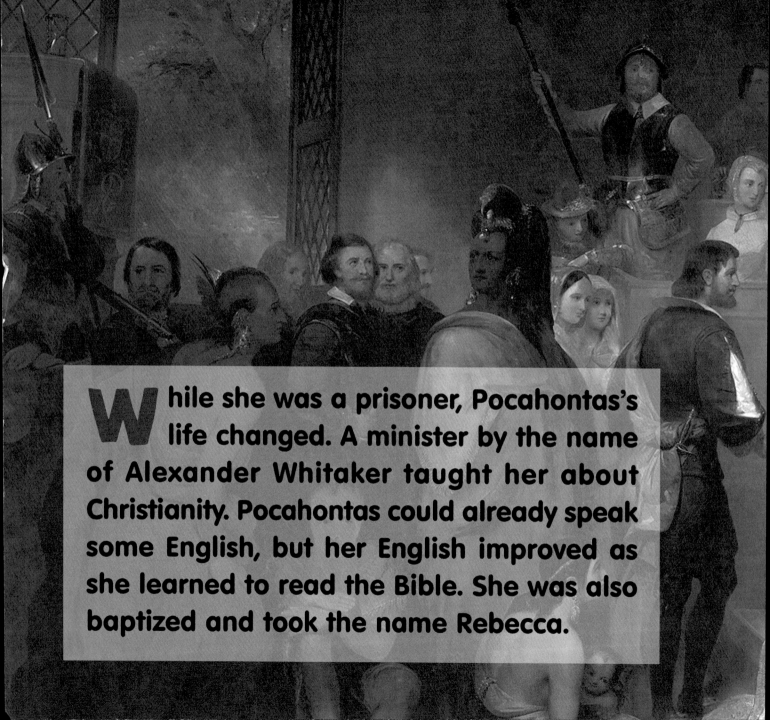

While she was a prisoner, Pocahontas's life changed. A minister by the name of Alexander Whitaker taught her about Christianity. Pocahontas could already speak some English, but her English improved as she learned to read the Bible. She was also baptized and took the name Rebecca.

BAPTISM OF POCAHONTAS

In the Bible, Rebecca was the mother of two sons who established two different nations, so the name may have been selected because Pocahontas was between two worlds as well.

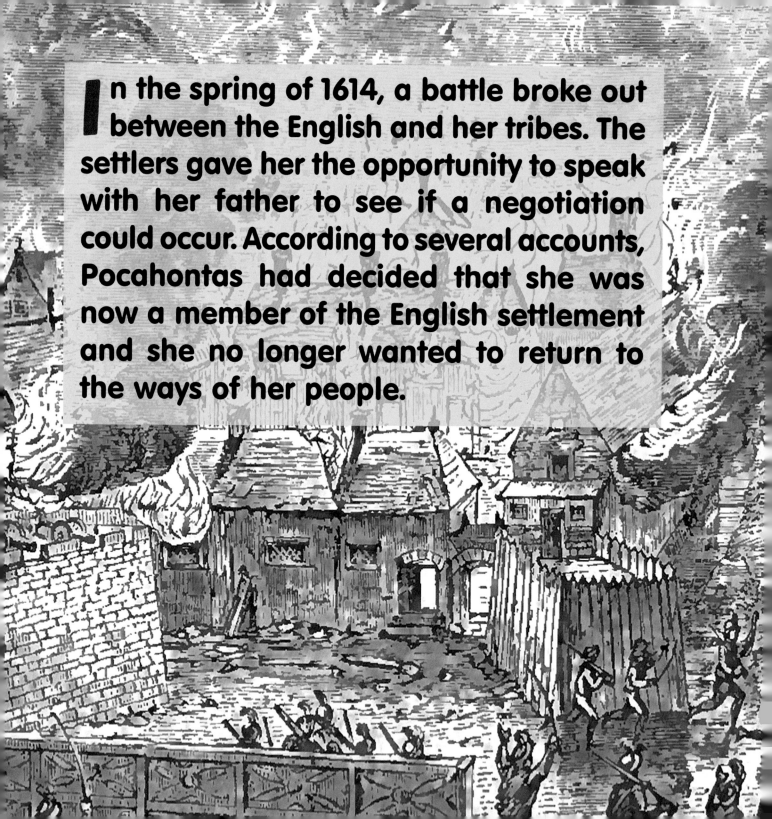

In the spring of 1614, a battle broke out between the English and her tribes. The settlers gave her the opportunity to speak with her father to see if a negotiation could occur. According to several accounts, Pocahontas had decided that she was now a member of the English settlement and she no longer wanted to return to the ways of her people.

JOHN ROLFE AT THE FARM

Perhaps part of the reason for this was because she had met John Rolfe during the time she was in captivity. Prior to his journey across the Atlantic from England, Rolfe, who was a good, religious man, had lost his wife and his child.

THE MARRIAGE OF POCAHONTAS

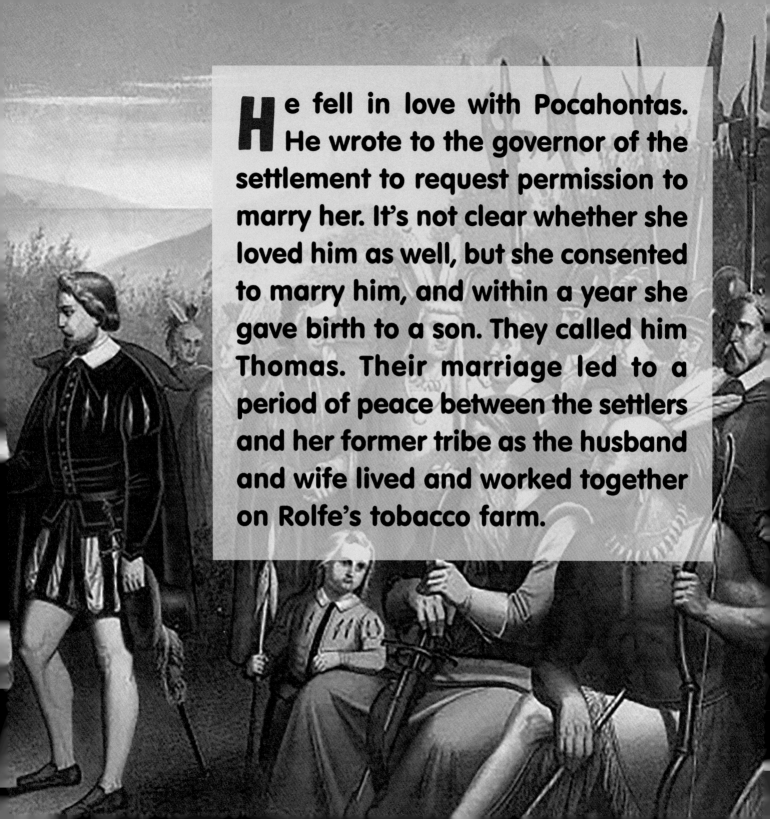

He fell in love with Pocahontas. He wrote to the governor of the settlement to request permission to marry her. It's not clear whether she loved him as well, but she consented to marry him, and within a year she gave birth to a son. They called him Thomas. Their marriage led to a period of peace between the settlers and her former tribe as the husband and wife lived and worked together on Rolfe's tobacco farm.

THE ROLFES TRAVEL TO ENGLAND

The Virginia Company was a group of investors who were creating new settlements in Virginia. Part of their "mission" was to convert the pagan Native Americans to Christianity. They saw Pocahontas as a symbol of this type of conversion. Pocahontas and her husband were offered a trip to England, which they agreed to take.

GROUP OF NATIVE AMERICANS

POCAHONTAS DRESSED IN FINE CLOTHES

Pocahontas was treated well in England and the Virginia Company presented her as a native "princess" who had been converted to Christianity. She dressed in fine clothes and was introduced to the king and other dignitaries in January of 1617. Then, something surprising happened. Captain John Smith was at one of the events and sought her out. This meeting was difficult for Pocahontas because she had thought her friend was dead. Once she got over the trauma of seeing him, she was angry about how the English had treated her father and her tribe. She reminded John of all the good deeds she and others had done for him and the other settlers.

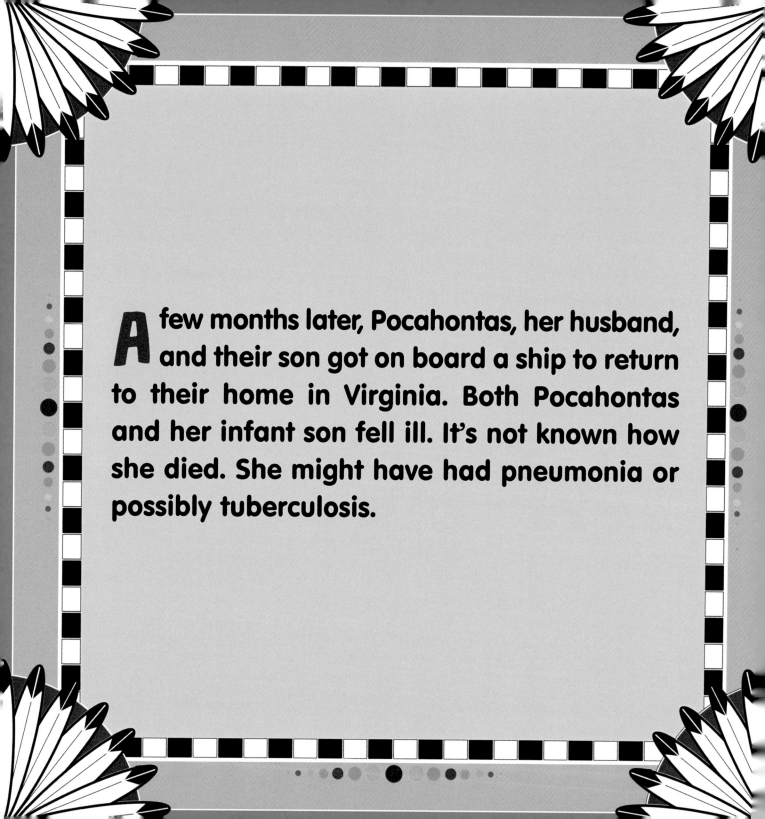

A few months later, Pocahontas, her husband, and their son got on board a ship to return to their home in Virginia. Both Pocahontas and her infant son fell ill. It's not known how she died. She might have had pneumonia or possibly tuberculosis.

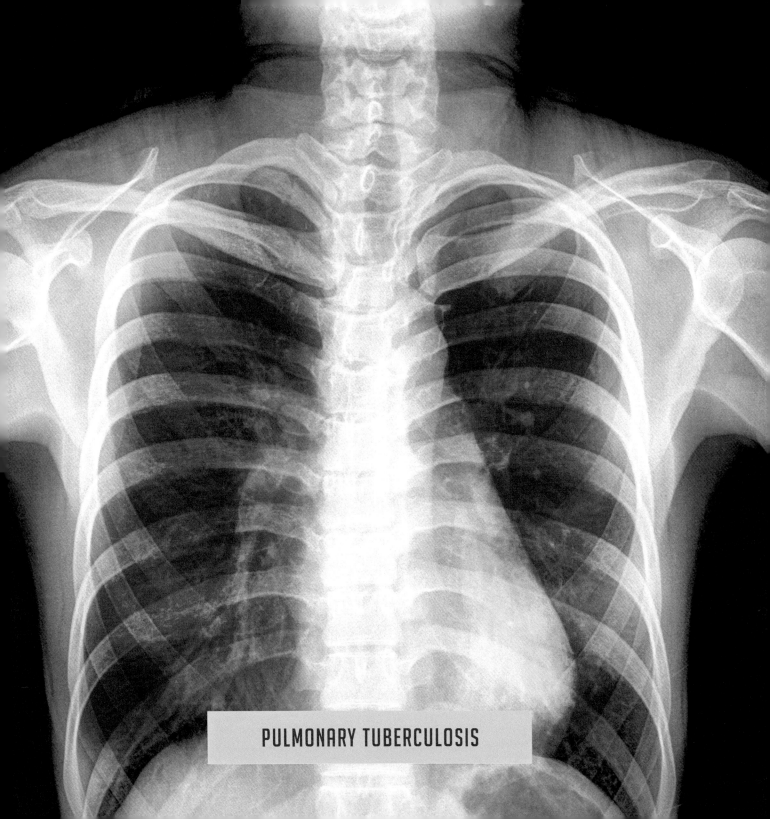

PULMONARY TUBERCULOSIS

POCAHONTAS AND HER SON

She was only twenty-two years old. Her husband went back to Virginia, but never saw their son again. Thomas was too ill to travel back and stayed in England for a long time. Thomas Rolfe eventually came back to America and many established families in Virginia claim to be descendants of his family.

Now you know more about the life of Pocahontas. You can find more Biography books from Baby Professor by searching the website of your favorite book retailer.

Visit

BABY PROFESSOR
EDUCATION KIDS

www.BabyProfessorBooks.com

to download Free Baby Professor eBooks and view
our catalog of new and exciting Children's Books